Let's Fall in Love

A True-Life Fairy Tale

And Insights for Other Senior Romantics

By
Kathleen and Bob Carroll

Copyright ©2020 By Kathleen Carroll and Bob Carroll

All rights reserved.
No part of this book may be reproduced, scanned,
or distributed in any printed or electronic form,
without express written permission from the author.

ISBN: 978-1-939237-73-6

Illustrated by Allison Daigle

Published by Suncoast Digital Press, Inc.
Sarasota, Florida, USA
suncoastdigitalpress.com

Dedication and Thanks

To the cupids of our love affair ~

Dick Chegar, Dianne Avlon, Bill Regnery,
Janet Page, Len Ferraguzzi, and Nicole Pridgen

Introduction

We are writing this book for our family and friends because we believe it is a unique, fun and wonderful love story.

In Part I of the book, we spin our romantic yarn in a section titled "Fairy Tales Do Come True!" Our love story is written as a fairy tale, but it all really did happen. It really did!

We are also writing this book to share with others our experience of finding and courting someone on social media. We know of a number of people who have become single later in life, who very much want to find a new partner and who simply do not know how. Most are lonely, many exasperated and some depressed. These people have not met anyone in their circle of friends, and few seem to be able to use dating sites to meet a soulmate. Others have an outright fear of the unknowns of internet connecting.

In Part II of the book, our experiences are documented in a section titled "Insights For Senior Romantics, Like Us."

It all started on January 21, 2019, when these curious and cryptic messages appeared on our computers via Match.com:

Kat	Bob
72 • Charleston, SC	78 • Englewood, FL
Seeking men 64 - 80	Seeking women 65 - 75

Thence began our journey with mantra and favorite song,

"Let's Fall In Love"

Part I

Fairy Tales Do Come True!

Chapter One

Once upon a time...
In a land far away where older people live (grandparents and people like that,) there was a woman (Kathleen) and a man (Bob) who lived in totally different worlds. They were in fact light years apart from each other by physical distance, (thousands of furlongs, as the raven flies), age, social connections, education, kingdoms and even common interests.

Let's call them for now, The Princess and The Soldier.

They each lived by the sea but on other sides of a great land.

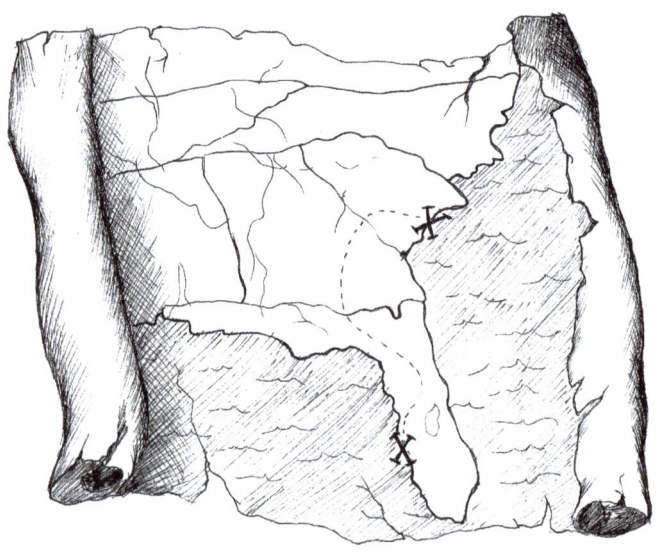

The Princess lived a hoity~toity lifestyle in an elegant kingdom with big castles where magnolia trees and swaying palms grew side by side and people made much ado about museums and symphonies and about the refinement of their clothes and their seated dinner parties with fine wines. Conversations among the lords and ladies centered on the treasury of the kingdom and the fluctuations of the gold reserves. Her vassals all felt they were far superior to subjects of other far~away lands.

The Soldier also lived at waterside but in a more rustic setting. His quarters were in a jungle campsite with a garden of flowers he had planted in honor of his late wife. His life was casual and kicked~back and simple. Entertaining involved pot~luck suppers with tankards of ale, dancing a Celtic jig some nights at the local lodge, much mirth and merriment and boat outings on a lovely quiet bay.

The Soldier's life as a military officer had led him halfway around the world serving his liege. He had graduated from a military school steeped in the spartan tradition and then led knights on a far~away crusade to a distant land called Viet Nam. This brave knight had won the Order of the Silver Star along the way, earned two masters degrees, taught leadership at the land's most prestigious school for knights (West Point) and then coached other knights to be brave.

His interests were teaching, writing, dancing and riding on a newfangled contraption called a bicycle. His status and prestige lay not necessarily in the small bags of gold he had amassed but in the assets he had stored up of integrity, honesty, fealty and leadership. His feudal ambition was to guard, not to gain.

The Princess, on the other hand, in spite of early decision acceptance to the Wellesley School for brainy princesses, had dropped out of school to be married at age nineteen, begat two wonderful children, divorced, remarried and then divorced again. Her path had been a jagged zigzag of adventure, learning and exotic travels. Her passions were collecting works of art, decorating castles, and entertaining with all her finery.

Chapter Two

In January of a certain year, somehow the Soldier and the Princess had each fallen into the well… the proverbial well of exasperation and loneliness.

The Soldier had been a widower for some three years and, in spite of dating lots of friends of friends and damsels in distress, felt frustrated and lonelier than ever. He wondered how he would ever meet someone compatible and fun.

The Princess was also at her wits' end. An on~again, off~again romance had ended several months before and having been without a prince for almost fifteen years, she was giving up on the idea of ever finding someone who could mirror her joie de vivre, kind spirit, and sense of fun and adventure and someone who could make her laugh at any hour of the day or night. The last trait was key.

She had searched for years for a prince who met all of her royal requirements for princely education, lofty titles, chests of gold, and exclusive castle memberships. The track she had been on was getting her nowhere towards her goal of finding a lifelong companion. In spite of her successful reign and the support of her loving family, she felt somehow a failure that she could not settle down with a proper and loving consort.

So, in desperation, the Princess sought the help of a renowned matchmaking wizard who immediately challenged her search criteria. "Why are you seeking such superficial traits?" the wizard challenged. "Why don't you search for the heart of the matter?"

The princess raised one eyebrow quizzically, "What do you mean by that?" Whereupon the wizard expounded on searching for character not credentials on Match.com.

Meanwhile, the Soldier had been rewriting his own script for Match.com with the help of a daughter-in-law, who encouraged him to include pictures of his travels to Mongolia and Russia.

He included pictures to show his humane and down-to-earth side with his family. He also tossed in a picture of himself in his most worthy costume, replete with all his feudal crests and battle ribbons. (Of course, this would be the shot to captivate the Princess's eye!)

Being confident in his magnetism as a handsome, fit, accomplished Soldier, he limited his search to very close territory. As he searched, in spite of turning up dozens of beautiful maidens, he was left feeling incomplete and not heading in the right direction.

Chapter Three

And so,
it was after Christmas of this particular year, during the desolate, dreary days of January, when the Princess was ready to throw in the crown and pull up the drawbridge forever, that she noticed a very handsome Soldier who appeared on the frontier of her Match.com. His profile was forthright and warm and his pictures eye~catching. Some of his pictures were a bit frightening in their quirkiness, but others completely captivating in the spirit and charm they exuded.

"Hmmm," she said to herself, "he lives far outside my realm but there seems something different about this man." So she sent him a brief missive~~ very brief, not wanting to embarrass herself should he not be interested. She greatly feared rejection but was eager as always for adventure. She had been in the doldrums too long and was now more than ever determined to fall in love with the perfect match.

However, as the Soldier looked at the Match.com site, the Soldier took note! "What an odd picture for a princess," he thought. "she seems so commonplace in a straw hat and so simple, but her regal profile claims that she is broadly traveled and well~read~~ maybe even interesting?"

He, too, was bogged down in the gloominess of January and thought maybe a princess in a straw hat might be down to earth enough for a Soldier to meet, possibly even amusing and entertaining. Besides, he thought to himself, she had a beautiful smile.

Chapter Four

And so began the strangest of courtships.

A Princess approaching a Soldier on Match.com with the most mundane of all mundane sentences, "You seem nice."

And the Soldier responding brilliantly, "You have a nice smile."

Then reaching for some profound level of dialogue, he asked, "Where did you get that smile?"

Cleverly, she replied, "I think I was just born with it."

Slowly, over time, the conversation relaxed, the openness grew and the online relationship began to develop.

Soon after the first internet exchange, to the Princess's utter surprise, the Soldier (who quickly became intrigued to say the least by this faraway royalty who seemed to have more to her than just being a high~fallutin princess) began an all~out "forced march" to meet the Princess and to capture her hand.

The two were separated by many days ride from the newly settled frontier village of Englewood where the Soldier lived to the ancient and aristocratic city of Charleston where the Princess lived. The Soldier determined that the only way to get to know each other was first to talk by phone but then to connect on Facetime where they could look into each other's eyes and experience the warmth of each other's smile.

After a few days of telephoning, the charismatic and charming Soldier convinced the Princess to see one another on Facetime.

Now you must realize, the Princess did not know or favor the idea of Facetime. She was accustomed to having people come face~to~face to HER, traveling great distances, bearing gifts and compliments and to all audiences being arranged on her terms. And she communicated this in no uncertain terms to the Soldier. Yet, in spite of this edict the Soldier insisted on setting up a Facetime date.

When the date of the Facetime came, it did not suit the Princess at all (for she was having a VERY bad hair day and had packed gunk on her frizzy golden locks), and she was shocked and a bit put off when the Soldier called her anyway!

She had plainly told him this did not suit. But he had not obeyed! This was decidedly out of line. When he called, she yelled "Argh! I told you today does not suit!"

However, the Soldier was so handsome and so winsome and so warm, that a tiny section of the Princess's heart melted that very first Facetime. She soon found herself wanting to talk to the Soldier over and over and over again and falling under the spell of the Soldier's smile, deep blue eyes and wily words of desire to meet in person and to woo her.

The Soldier himself was in shock. He had been in battles with bullets whizzing over his helmet and horse. He had moved mountains to move legions of men. He had tackled raising two wonderful sons and changing careers, but he had never met someone (on Facetime no less!) who had pierced the armor of his vulnerability in quite such a way.

Within days the Soldier was using his most powerful weapon (his way with words) with the Princess. He told her he couldn't believe it but he was falling in love in spite of never having met her.

Alas, the Princess was feeling the same way. However, having been brought up to be skeptical and standoffish and to play hard-to-get, she kept up her guard in spite of the Soldier's strong desire to see her in person and to have her go to far away Florida, which she absolutely refused to do. The Soldier knew that if he wanted to win her, he would have to travel (no matter how far) to find her and to impress her with whatever talents he had.

And so the Soldier crafted a plan. One that would take him to Charleston. He was known far and wide for the excellence of his highly structured planning of military operations.

He used this talent to craft an operation plan (OPLAN) for this romance. He brought all of his tactical and strategic skills to create "OPLAN ROMANCE."

His plan was to move very slowly and honorably and very, very carefully, realizing that princesses required lots and LOTS of courting and proof of a suitor's intent. He wanted to make sure that this campaign was highly successful and its outcome long lasting and solid.

Now, while the Soldier was putting the final touches on OPLAN ROMANCE, the Princess continued to examine his pictures on Match.com and fear trickled down her delicate regal spine that there might be an outlandish side to this Soldier that would knock her right off her balcony.

There was the much-feared red suit, and the Michael Jackson costume and mention of tap-dancing classes!

Was this Soldier a real Soldier or an erstwhile performer for a traveling minstrel show? She was confused, but so smitten by the captivating courtship that she could not slow the momentum of her feelings.

Chapter Five

The Soldier's OPLAN began to work. Little by little his wooing (sending her a giant Valentine and a gorgeous bouquet of flowers, tracking down friends of hers and wowing them with his charm) was impressing the heck out of the Princess. Her resistance was breaking down. After some forty hours of Facetime with the handsome Soldier, she was now addicted to seeing him and talking with him over her morning cappuccino and evening chalice of wine.

On the first of March she agreed for him to make his frontal assault and to visit her in her kingdom. Strict rules and regulations would apply: little or no physical contact and of course he would not stay at the castle but at some predetermined and nearby encampment of his choice. The strategic engagement was about to begin in full force and nerves on both sides were strung tight!

Elaborate preparations went into effect in readiness for the Soldier's arrival.

The Princess was in a frenzy! A new wardrobe was certainly a must but what kind? She had always been an elegant dresser, but she wanted to look exceptional on this special day. In the past the Princess had always sought out only the finest, the most stylish, in fact the most expensive, but suddenly felt such a wardrobe was all out of whack. What good was a Gucci belt or Hermes scarf for impressing a Soldier whose focus was on character and compassion, not on alligator skins and silk? She would have to alter her course. And the Princess was used to calling the shots. Now she was letting her empathy step in. This was preposterous... What next?

The Soldier began the long journey, and the Princess changed gowns a dozen times searching for the perfect combination to wow the wooer.

She abandoned her chauffeured chariot and drove herself to the outskirts of her kingdom to await in the cell parking lot (imagine that!) with her nerves on edge.

She was not accustomed to waiting for others and all this drove her wild with desire to be held in the Soldier's embrace. She knew he had a strict OPLAN to allow the romance to grow slowly and surely, but the Princess had never gone by anyone else's rules... ever. .. never... ever... only hers!

Finally, thirty~nine days after their first Match.com message, the Soldier arrived, riding his favorite steed, Jet Blue.

Dressed in simple britches, cloak and hat~not in the glamorous uniform of battle with shiny helmet, full mail coat and lance that she had expected.

But still her heart was pounding. She was bound by the parameters of the OPLAN to receive the Soldier's deep bow with her discreet curtsy, perhaps even a light kiss on the cheek. Instead, in a moment of uncontrollable excitement and passion, the Princess (in front of dozens of subjects!) planted the kiss of a lifetime on the lips of the Soldier who was in total disbelief!

Did he not remember Sleeping Beauty and how it took the passionate kiss of a prince to awaken her from a hundred years of sleep? The Princess had no idea if the Soldier had even been sleeping, but she was darn sure going to wake him up. And wake him up she did!

The Soldier was speechless and dumbfounded that at this first meeting the Princess was not obeying the OPLAN. The Soldier went to place his knap sack into her carriage when a commoner standing next to her traveling trunk exclaimed, "It is my most fervent wish that someday upon arrival home after a long journey to receive a kiss like that."

Whereupon the Soldier turned to the amused bystanders and said, "Would you like to meet her? I just met her, myself!"

And so began the first date. A Soldier with an OPLAN, and a Princess throwing all sheets to the wind and opening her heart up yet again to the possibility and the intention of falling in love. None of this made sense~yet they each moved forward with some solid belief that "this is it!" This sentiment formed the basis for their mission and their favorite song, "Let's Fall in Love!"

Rules had been written to be followed but were soon abandoned. Eventually the Soldier moved from his campsite into the castle and decided to spend an extra day before returning home to his bayside retreat. He had wondered before if he was truly smitten, but now he was sure. Match.com and Facetime had brought him his dream.

Back and forth they traveled, the beautiful Princess and the handsome Soldier. They toured the coastline near the edge of the great sea and attended a jousting contest at a neighboring city.

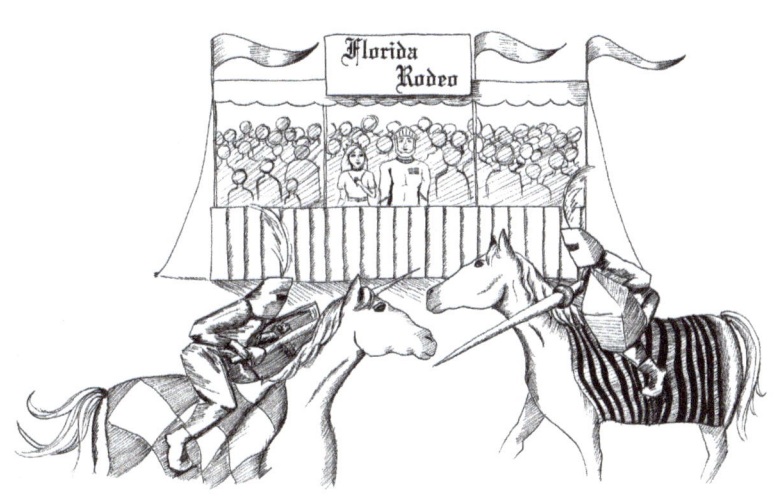

Becoming acquainted with their different kingdoms and forts, they soon realized that those material aspects were not what sealed the attraction. There was something else deeper...a love of dancing? A love of families? A love of discussing current events? Gazing into each other's eyes? What was it?

The wizard had worked her spell. It was magic for sure!

Chapter Six

The Soldier was now determined to spend the rest of his life with this Princess whom he scarcely knew. She had never felt such persistence but loved every minute of it... in fact, she was falling head over heels!

Soon plans were made to visit the Princess's favorite kingdom on earth, Paris... but also, to include a visit to one of the Soldier's favorite battlefields on earth, Normandy... the French Duchy from whence the Soldier's Norman ancestors had launched an attack by small boats across the channel in 1066. (Much later their descendants would do likewise in the other direction in 1944.)

At this point, the fairy tale took a dangerous turn. The Soldier did not want to take his eyes off the Princess... even for a minute much less a few days. So before taking the adventurous voyage to Paris, he inadvertently mentioned possibly visiting her later in the summer at her mountain castle.

"Alas!" said the Princess. "That simply will not work."

"What???" exclaimed the Soldier. "But I do not want to be apart from you!"

The Princess furrowed her wide tall forehead and announced that no princess ever allowed a Soldier (or even a prince for that matter) to dwell with her without solemn obligations. Heaven forbid!

So the Soldier, wise romantic that he was, immediately knew what he must do. He sought out the most famous beloved jeweler in all the Princess's kingdom and lay forth the command to find the most beautiful diamond ring that ever the Princess could imagine. Never mind the difficulty or the cost~after all this was a Princess. The Soldier could always sell his sword and steed to pay for the darn thing! He wanted the best, and it must be a ring that would dazzle even a princess into saying "YES!" should a proposal of engagement be forthcoming.

Of course, get the ring the Soldier did. And carried it in humble crinkled paper in his riding britches all the way to Paris to await the perfect moment (in a tiny cafe on la Rive Gauche complete with a violinist, the first violinist of the Paris Symphony no less) to get down on one knee and profess his love to his Princess and to ask for her hand in marriage. (It was one hundred and eleven days since they had first met on Match.com.)

For the first time in her life, The Princess was speechless. Her eyes were blinded by the elegance and beauty of the ring and by the love and devotion of the Soldier and by his crystal~clear blue eyes...so when her consciousness returned, she said "Oui! Mais oui!"

And now the Princess and the Soldier are living happily ever after, proving to the world that it is possible for two elderly subjects of two vastly different kingdoms, subjects who once lived very, very far apart, to fall in love through Match.com and Facetime and to prove that fairy tales do come true!!

The End

No, not the end,
and not the beginning.

The end of the beginning!

Part II

Insights for
Other Senior Romantics

A. Are You Game?

- People later in life who become single for whatever reason can become very lonely and even depressed.
- Grandparents and other senior citizens are not too old to fall in love.
- People looking for romance later in life possess a treasure of rich and varied experiences, many involving a former spouse, a family, and children. Former lives and relationships are part of the package. This could present a challenge or offer a rich opportunity.

B. Mindset

- A sense of humor is essential. Being able to laugh at oneself and with a partner is powerful fuel for falling in love.
- It helps to have a clear idea in one's mind that the goal is to fall in love and to have a life partner. Looking just for a date will expand possibilities but this is only the first step to finding a soulmate.
- As a senior, it is wise not to let grass grow under one's feet. The endeavor to find a partner should be pursued with cautious speed. Bob's son asked him if he wasn't going too fast, to which Bob replied, "Do you know how old I am?" Some refer to this as "Tick Tock."
- Finding the proper soulmate may require getting out of the proverbial comfort zone, out of the box. This involves taking risks. With internet dating there are ample ways to protect one's privacy, name, email, telephone number, address and physical security. The risk referred to here is risk to the heart, risk to take a chance, risk to be rejected, risk to fall in love.

- People currently sixty or over were brought up with the man taking the lead. It is fine for the woman to convey the first introductory message, but the man needs to be the pursuer. And this means an aggressive lead. Should he not, the woman may feel unwanted. Moreover, the man has to be assertive and creative in his wooing. Think of flowers, candy, cards etc. Carpe Diem. Bob's mom, a very wise woman, had always said, "A man chases a woman until she catches him."

C. Carefully Prescribe Your Search

- It will greatly limit one's success to search only within a tight circle of friends, social groups, churches, clubs, hangouts and geography.
- A potential soulmate can come from an unexpected location and have a distinctly different background.
- It is easy to fall into the trap of searching for beauty, wealth, education or social status in one's partner instead of searching for similar values and outlook on life.

D. Be Open

- Senior citizens have had a lifetime to get set in their ways. Some might say ossified! It is very helpful to get flexible in habits and routines in order to adapt to a partner's lifestyle. And this again is a two-way street. Annoyance and frustration must be replaced by tolerance and amusement.
- It sounds basic but being real is essential. It is too easy to get hung up on what one looks like and what image to present.
- Quirkiness in a potential partner might evolve from a warning signal to something of interest and fun. It will pay dividends to keep a sense of humor. Stay curious!

E. *Match.com:* A Senior's Tutorial

- Match.com is called a "dating site," but this is a misnomer. Many people are not just looking for a date; they are looking for a life partner.

- A lot of people on these dating sites and other sites are simply looking for someone to contact. There are surely some who are even out to scam or harm. But this medium can help sort through and weed out the suitors and allow a person to get to know someone quite well, long before meeting for coffee, a drink, or a supper.

- On a site like Match.com, people create a profile consisting of a lead photo (normally a head shot), a short article describing what the person is like and what the person is looking for, and additional or back-up photos. Searching on these sites, Bob and Kathleen were both attracted to each other's variety of pictures, openness, vulnerability, honesty, and sense of humor.

- It is a good thing to be cautious of people lying, using dated photos, or not being very open in their profiles. Those who only put one picture or describe their life in one sentence are bound to be shallow. Sunglasses conceal the face; hats on men can imply a desire to cover up baldness; head-only shots do not display physical appearance and fitness.

- The dating web site uses algorithms to link people of similar ages, backgrounds, interests, and tastes. (Bob had been searching within a 90-mile radius; Kathleen had broadened hers to 500. This explains why Bob's picture showed up on Kathleen's computer and not vice versa.)

- Note the built-in security of the site: In our case, Kathleen used a nickname of "Kat" and no last name, home address, telephone number or email address. In this way she controlled all message traffic. All Bob knew was that he had a gorgeous gal named Kat from Charleston who liked him.

- Over time and with permission, communications can open up and expand from the web site, to email, to telephone, to Facetime (a lot of Facetime) and finally to a personal visit to meet. Both the woman and the man have the power to avoid those suitors in whom they have no interest.

- Moreover, the gradual and measured increase of comunication and openness allow a relationship to build in a very safe and fun way.

F. *Facetime:* A Senior's Tutorial

- Most seniors are familiar with Facetime or Skype as mainly for keeping in contact with grandchildren. For the uninitiated, a smart phone with a (free) Facetime application allows one to connect visually over the telephone. In addition to hearing each other speak, one sees the face of the person called or calling.

- This app is essential to move the older generation into the 21st century and a wonderful tool when searching for life-partners. It allows participants to see facial expressions, personality, comportment, lifestyle. As one person speaks and opens up, the other really gets to know that person quite well before asking for or accepting any date.

- Two people can really get to know each other on Facetime, but it takes time, commitment, openness and desire. And two to tango. Both must really show up. (We used Facetime extensively, daily, over morning coffee and evening wine. We talked about everything under the sun and above it. We estimate we communicated some 40 hours over Facetime in the first month. That is tantamount to five or six dates in person. Facetime set the scene for our first meeting.)

G. Meetings

- Especially for your first meeting, bring along a healthy sense of humor. Even if the date goes haywire, you might come away with a funny story to tell later.
- Meeting friends of one's new partner can be nerve-racking. There is most certainly an ongoing vetting process at work. The only way to be is to be oneself. No airs.
- Meeting each other's children is crucial. Of course, they want the best for the older couple, but they often have a strong attachment to the former spouse. They will naturally be suspicious. They have to see the seniors exuding love.
- Children may downplay that they wonder how a potential new marriage will affect their inheritance. Share with them the intent of any prenuptial agreement.

H. Commitment

- In some cases, the couple may want to sanctify their relationship with some form of ceremony. If not, the couple will just be "living together," which may be OK for some. Not for others.
- Another option is just an engagement with no clear commitment or path to marriage. Many discard that idea, thinking that engagement means a real commitment to get married.
- The other option is engagement and marriage.
- The man often wants the engagement to be a surprise. (With a sense of tradition, Bob confided with Kathleen's two children that he intended to ask for her hand. Kathleen's father being long deceased, Bob still received permission to propose.)

- The ring is an outward and visible sign of a deep commitment. This is a big deal for most couples, but especially so for older couples on second or third marriages. Some fall into the trap of economizing on the ring, a bad idea. A worse idea, use an old one from the jewelry box.
- Give some thought to picking a memorable spot to propose. It is a huge event, and with great optimism it will be the last marriage proposal in this lifetime.

Finally, it helps to laugh a lot. And to just keep on laughing. Life is too short to allow petty disagreements to spoil the fun.

Good luck,

Kathleen & Bob

Profile from match.com, January 21, 2019

Kat 72 • Charleston, SC • Seeking men 64 - 80

For me...all the adventures and all the every-day pleasures are doubled if sharing with someone. Seeking romance and love with a man who has led a sophisticated life who wants to continue life adventures with someone who is energetic, curious, fun and adventurous.

I enjoy honest, true, fun loving people. A good sense of humor and being able to laugh at oneself are the keys to a happy life to me.

Having grown up in the South, I love all things southern, but am open minded towards all types of people and places. Attended college in Boston, spent a summer as an exchange student in Italy and have traveled the world. . ..England, France, Greece, Turkey, Morocco, Bangkok, China, Australia and New Zealand among others. I have never been on safari in Africa. . ..a trip I so wish to make, but am longing to go with a best friend and lover.

I love to be in the country hunting but also like to play golf and to watch golf, football, basketball and other sports on TV or live. Other passions are art, antiques, music, dancing, good wine and fine dining.

My family - two fantastic grown children and four grandchildren - is important to me and I stay in touch with them as much as possible.

Hoping so much to meet someone who is kind first and foremost and who is comfortable with himself. . ..someone who is generous. . ..loves to laugh and have fun. . .likes adventure. . .enjoys art and music and fine dining equally as well as eating a barbecue sandwich from a great dive on a country road. Certainly someone who is highly intelligent and enjoys lively and expanding discussions on everything from books recently read to world economics.

Profile from match.com, January 21, 2019

Bob 78 • Englewood, FL • Seeking women 65–75

Hi. I decided NOT to lie about my age. I don't just look younger, I AM a lot younger, in spirit. Active and athletic, with no disabilities, thank God. My weekly routine includes bicycling, swimming, tap and ballroom dancing. I see myself as a gentleman, healthy, fit, and not-too-old. So please read on.

My wonderful wife of 43 years died in 2016. I have recently taken out a number of very nice ladies. Thus far, I have not found the long-term partner with whom I want to travel and share an intimate and fun-filled life. So, I reluctantly decided to overcome my reservations and enter the abyss of this dating site.

Whom am I looking for? I've discovered that I am attracted to wonderful smiles, especially when they are aimed at me and especially when the smiles are laughing at something funny or dumb I have said. I greatly admire well-read and well-travelled women, aware of the amazing politics of the US and the world. I hope my future partner is sociable and can assist in hosting my friends and hers for parties large and small. She has to love my family, but that will be no problem. Both of my wonderful boys married "up" (as did I) and have given me three gorgeous grandkids. We regularly link up at their homes in New Mexico, San Francisco, or chez moi. From my Ranger experience, I built a zip line into my pool, which the kids adore.

I retired after three careers (military, banking, consulting). Grew up in DC; lived in Georgia, New York, Hawaii, Colorado, Ohio, France, Germany, and, oh yes, Vietnam. I recently published a book on leadership. Because evenings are so lonely, I go out dancing a lot. (I may do the best jitterbug in SW FL.)

As do most of us on this site, I promote myself as socially outgoing, financially solvent, physically fit, of high integrity, compassionate, great character, trustworthy, and rather sexy. I might add: legally not under surveillance. If you haven't divined it yet, I have a great sense of humor. Please let me know if you are interested. In the meantime, happy hunting. Bob C.

www.ingramcontent.com/pod-product-compliance
Lightning Source LLC
Chambersburg PA
CBHW061743290426
43661CB00127B/962